I0416330

Mother, Heal Your Child

Techniques for anyone to help another

by

Wayne C. Irwin

Doctor of Metaphysics
Doctor of Hypnotherapy

Third Edition

ISBN: 1-4107-0465-3 (e-book)
ISBN: 1-4107-0466-1 (Paperback)
ISBN: 1-4107-0467-X (Dust Jacket)

Library of Congress Control Number: 2002096616

This book is printed on acid free paper.

Printed in the United States of America
Bloomington, IN

1stBooks – rev. 03/21/03

Also by this author

Learning The Psychic Shift
A Self-Training Guide for
Directed Intuition

To avoid an incessant, disruptive "him or her"
in discussions, this book employs the
masculine convention for most
third-person pronouns.

Foreword To Third Edition
(2003)

This third edition expands the therapeutic "read-aloud-from-the-book" contents that were praised so highly by Dr. Bryan in his foreword to the first edition (which follows). The book now contains treatments for additional aspects of attitude, behavior, and problems that may respond to this method, including illnesses.

The added material includes such diverse topics as speedy recovery from injury or illness, improved confidence during public appearances, standing alone against peer pressure, avoiding smoking, and reduction of prejudice.

With rising costs for medical and other professional services, and their limited availability in many areas of this and other countries, any valid home remedy — such as those offered in these pages — can be a godsend to many of those in need, and the book was devised for that purpose.

As my drawing on the cover implies, the explanatory text is directed primarily to a mother in caring for her child. However, the wording of the actual verbal treatments are designed to be equally beneficial for anyone, child or adult, and can be provided by anyone who can read aloud in the manner described.

To make the book easier to use in dim lighting, as is beneficial in some cases for consideration of the "patient," who may be asleep, the print is enlarged in the selections to be read aloud.

Nothing in this book is intended to replace appropriate medical or other professional help when needed.

The Author

Foreword To First Edition
(1972)

Having devoted the better part of a lifetime to the treatment of patients with psychoneurotic, psychosomatic and emotional ills, and being the first physician in the United States to specialize full-time in medical hypnosis, I perhaps realize more than most the value of a book which is largely devoted to preventative medicine.

While it is extremely important to cure cases of mental and emotional illnesses as they present themselves to the physician, it is perhaps even more important to prevent such illness before it starts, if this can be done.

Freud pointed out many years ago that the vast majority of neuroses begin in childhood. This is true primarily because children have little or no defense against traumatic events, which are likely to place negative suggestions in their subconscious minds.

The author of this book has laid down a set of suggestions which, if repeatedly given to a child, will certainly be likely to strengthen that child's mental and emotional defenses. In fact, W. C. Irwin has created with this book a sort of mental vaccination against many of the traumas and mental diseases to which children are susceptible.

For this reason, it is a book that every mother will want to read and should have.

It will also be useful to psychologists, psychiatrists, hypnotechnicians and others who may be treating children for emotional illnesses, and who may wish to brush up on their semantics and reword some of their direct suggestions.

That this book is good is proof that one does not have to be a medical doctor in order to come up with a good therapeutic suggestion. In fact, many of the great discoveries in medicine have been by men who were other than in the medical profession. Chemists, physicists, bacteriologists, immunologists, electronic engineers and countless others in many and varied professions have joined the medical profession in their war on disease.

I hope that this book will be a pretty big cannon in waging that war.

William J. Bryan, Jr.
M.D., J.D., Ph.D., LL.D.,
F.A.I.H., F.A.C.M.H.
Executive Director,
American Institute of Hypnosis

1972
Los Angeles, California

Contents

Part I

How The Technique Works

1.
Your Healing Voice

One of the most potent healing instruments known to man is the human voice. It has the power to comfort, to reassure, to cure, to inspire, to cause the attainment of perfection.

Equally, it can be terribly destructive.

The destructive influences can be seen readily about us, as angry voices char their victims, screeching voices tear at the mind, belittling voices gouge out the remnants of confidence and bring sickness to the discouraged.

This book deals with the positive use of the voice, its healing tone, its corrective energy. More precisely, it deals with one small area among the dynamics of verbal discipline — the area of factual encouragement through quiet repetition.

It tells you how, through the use of your own calm voice, to bring composure to your child, a release of tension from her mind, a resurgence of health to his body. It offers you aid in removing his fear and anxiety, her disease or debility.

You can also employ the same technique on any other person, for the method applies to everyone.

To do these things, you need no special learning, other than to be able to read aloud from the following pages in a pleasant tone of voice.

You need no special skill, other than to remove from your voice all harshness, strain, and concern.

You need no new viewpoint, other than to accept the truth of the principles involved.

And you can begin at once.

2.
Words Will Work

The healing power of therapeutic suggestion, presented by the spoken word, is well established, and there are many good books on the subject. It is not the purpose of this manual to restate the reasons why suggestion works, nor to offer persuasive evidence. It is sufficient to know that it does.

Rather, this book offers you collections of simple statements that have been found in therapy to be very beneficial.

Many of these phrases — referred to as "patter" — are words that you can speak to your child or other person to relax his or her mind and body, thereby removing the greatest single cause of diseases and impairments of all kinds — strain.

Such words are a natural curative for emotional stresses and are particularly effective in their removal. These stresses are intimately related to a child's general state of well-being.

As Dr. Rolf Alexander said in his book *The Doctor Alone Can't Cure You*, "Each emotional reaction, be it mild or severe, has immediate repercussions in every cell, tissue and function of the body."

---

* *The Doctor Alone Can't Cure You,* by Rolf Alexander, M.D. Published by MacAlester Park Publishing Company, Saint Paul, Minnesota, 1949.

As he explained in discussing the mechanism of illness, "It is therefore seen that the effects of fear, grief, worry and jealousy may not only aid disease by withdrawing energy from the repair function... but by reducing the alkaline potential of the blood, these harmful emotions actually indirectly speed the development of old diseases or help new ones to get started."

The patter phrases are beneficial because of their information content, not because of the formal schooling or professional affiliation of the person who speaks them.

Although an experienced therapist would be expected to be ordinarily more effective in their use than a layman, still the average person can achieve very good results with even a minimum of practice.

Further, because of the readiness of most children to accept reassuring words from their parents, there are times when a mother, father, or good friend may be even more effective than a professional within the range of applications given here.

Of course, for specific problems of either the mind or body, a professional in an appropriate field should be consulted, so that he or she may bring greater training and insight to bear upon the situation and diagnose the precise nature of the condition requiring treatment. This is especially true if the problem is aggravated.

You should not, for example, expect these elementary suggestions to be a solution to severe fevers and infections.

(There are very powerful methods of healing with the mind that can cure such difficulties nicely when employed by a person with sufficient skill, but this book does not deal with that subject.)

However, even for seriously disturbed children, the words presented in these pages can have strong remedial effect when read in a convincing manner. They are statements used by professional therapists.

The intent of the patter is to substitute ideas of a positive nature for those more negative ones currently in the child's mind. The idea of fatigue is replaced with one of relaxation, the idea of discouragement is replaced with one of cheer, the idea of sickness is replaced with one of health.

And as these new ideas are received by the subconscious mind, they displace the others, much as new information is fed into a computer.

These ideas make up a new reference against which the mind determines, in its ever-constant vigilance and evaluation, what adjustments and actions are appropriate for the physical body, the emotions, and the mental consciousness.

As the new information replaces the old, a new child emerges from the former.

You can assist in the shaping of that new child. You can have both immediate and far-ranging effects. You can contribute to the health and well-being of your child in a way you probably never thought possible. And it is very easy for you to do this.

All you have to do is select a patter suitable for your purpose and read it aloud to the child in the manner described.

The book is divided into four parts. This first one (chapters 1 through 6) explains the principles involved — the reasons the techniques work. The other three parts provide collections of patter designed for various purposes.

The patters in Part II are worded for benefits that can likely be achieved by simply eliminating strain. These sections apply to everyone.

Part III begins with three patters in Chapter 11 for maintaining or improving the general state of health and immune system response. Others in this grouping are appropriate for assisting in specific areas of physical health, such as speedy and easier recovery from injury or illness. The suggestions tailored to these specific purposes should be used in conjunction with the basic phrases for general health.

Part IV treatments are intended primarily for teenagers and adults, but are suitable for any age where they apply. They are designed to help with poor or unsatisfactory behavior or attitude — either temporary or on-going — for achieving objectives like strengthening resolve, avoiding smoking or drugs, and thinking clearly.

3.
But Keep In Mind

Naturally, as with any technique for doing anything, there are limitations to what can be accomplished with this method. Most of them are quite obvious to anyone with a little common sense.

As indicated in the previous chapter, you should not depend only upon a patter for relaxation when neither strain nor emotional disturbance is a significant part of the cause of the problem.

But even when strain and emotions are the source of trouble, there may be times when it would be wise for you to recognize that the difficulty is greater than you should try to cope with by yourself.

However, do not be too quick in selling yourself short. The method is sound, and with a little practice, you can become proficient and wonderfully effective in appropriate applications.

There is, though, one type of situation in which you might find yourself spinning your wheels. That would be if — perish the thought! — you are yourself instrumental in causing the stresses in your child that you now seek to remove with this patter. For if you are loading anxieties onto your child with your left hand and attempting to remove them with your right hand, it would be foolish to anticipate appreciable progress, regardless of what technique you use.

There are numerous ways that parents initiate, contribute to, or reinforce the anxieties of a child, ranging from indifference to emotional needs, to threats, to being a living example of someone who cannot be depended upon. These topics are not within the scope of this book with one exception, a particular form of anxiety-inducing behavior that is highly pertinent to this discussion.

And that is: **the way you use your voice**.

Just as your voice can be strikingly efficient in the removal of stresses, especially when employed as described on the following pages, so also can it become the single most damaging influence within a parent-child relationship.

Accordingly, the next chapter is devoted to reasons why you should know what you are doing when you open your mouth to speak. As stated so aptly in that humorous motto:

Warning: Do not engage mouth until brain is in motion.

4.
Mother, Lower Your Voice

These next remarks relate to the raising of your voice unnecessarily when communicating with your child.

Now, let's agree at the outset that there are times when raising the voice is proper and desirable, and in fact, even essential to the safety or life of your child. Or for that matter, when you are caught in the garage door and are calling for help. However, reasons of this sort are relatively few.

The other times the volume is increased above a conversational or instructional level become, by definition, unnecessary.

Certainly, when you are frustrated or angered half out of your mind, you may find yourself being seemingly forced into a louder tone. The word "unnecessary" is meant with respect to the desired objective and suitability of the voice for achieving that purpose, rather than to the operational commotion within which you find yourself enmeshed.

Thus, the concern here is not with how you can hope to remain calm. Instead, it is with the results that may occur if you do not. And these points are offered with frank recognition that there may be overriding reasons why it could be desirable in a particular circumstance to come out strongly with a verbal blast. (To speak of raising a child while lowering your voice probably appears to some to be a conflict of terms.)

One distinguishing characteristic about the unnecessary raising of a voice is that usually (but regrettably not always) it occurs unintentionally as a result of a person's becoming disturbed or excited in some way.

Of course, in a situation between antagonists, there is often a deliberate use of the voice as a weapon — to frighten, to confuse, to destroy. But any parent using a child as an antagonist by free choice would not be interested in employing this therapeutic patter for his benefit. So these combative purposes can be laid aside.

This leaves us still with a very sizeable collection of reasons for explosive outbursts — including anger, worry, bewilderment, fear, unhappiness, impatience, dislike.

When any such condition becomes a modifying influence upon your mode of speaking, the message is always distorted. For now the form of delivery has its own significance, and the strict semantic context of the message becomes colored by, and perhaps even submerged beneath, that which the emotions are spelling out so clearly.

From a metaphysical viewpoint, a loud voice, when caused by a negative emotion, has very damaging effect upon the child's "emotional body," which is one of the non-physical vehicles through which the human spirit experiences life on Earth.

More accurately, the parent's negative emotion itself strikes directly at the child.

The energies sent out by negative emotions and disturbed minds impinge against, and interfere with, the child's own energies and force fields on non-physical planes. This negativity disrupts the balance of emotions, impedes the smooth performance of the mental processes, and leads to impairment of physical functions.

Just as a word of love can make everything right, bringing a surge of happiness, confidence, and vitality to another, so can a harsh word cut him down and literally put him out of action.

In fact, no word need even be spoken, nor any sound made. The mere existence of a negative emotion or thought directed toward another person is enough to do the damage.

Only by consciously holding down and attempting to nullify the negative condition can the injury be lessened or prevented. Even with solid walls between the two persons, the energy of the vexation, anger, or hatred will flow unimpeded to smash at the recipient.

I once observed a habitually screaming mother berate her child for carelessly riding her tricycle into the street and coming uncomfortably close to being struck by a car. The mother was quite frightened, and — for an outlet for this distressful feeling — she turned upon her daughter with extreme intensity.

It might almost have been better if the car had grazed the child. At least, in that instance, the severity of the injury would have been recognized. And most people's physical bodies are better developed, a lot tougher, and much quicker to heal than their emotional bodies.

A little later, that same woman was screeching again at the girl for riding her tricycle a few houses down the street. *"Julie!! You get home this instant!"* Of course, Julie was not about to, because the unspoken message made it very clear that she wouldn't find any affection nor comfort at home.

The mother who shouts is also being harmed, because the emotional upset affects her own physical body.

As your emotions go out of tune, the harmony of your mind and body is shattered. If your reaction is of a kind that could be classed broadly as doing battle with the child, then your body gears itself to fight by pouring adrenalin into your bloodstream, thereby introducing changes and stresses that are not appropriate to the situation.

If these instances are frequent or prolonged, they alone may have severe impact on your health. And they certainly do observable harm to your peace of mind.

Your body works best and achieves most when you are relaxed and happy, and any kind of annoyance immediately renders such calmness impossible for longer periods than you might suppose.

If you happen to be one of those persons who never raises her voice because it is already always up there, then... Well... Let's go to the next point.

Your shouting may cause any of several negative responses within your child, or a combination. For instance:

- It may cause him to react with fear or goad him into an aggressive stance, with a resultant disturbance of chemical balance.

- It may cause him to erect a defensive shield between the two of you, shutting you out of his awareness.

- Or you may instill within him a sense of guilt, which is perhaps the most hurtful thing that one human can do to another without actually jeopardizing vital life functions or freedom of expression.

For guilt strikes at the feeling of self-worth and generally lasts for a lifetime — gnawing at the core of the personality — as the fear of discovery of past or present thoughts or actions destroys the person's full potential by inhibiting appropriate responses.

Depending upon how and why you elevate your tone, the undesirable impression received by your child may be one or more of the following. You can probably think up others.

- You may appear unfair. An abrupt manner is often enough by itself to create that image.

- You may seem to be cruel. A person subjected to harshness of tone may not give you the benefit of the doubt, even if capable of differentiating among the subtleties of various expressions.

- You may appear to be trying to humiliate. That would be another form of cruelty, ripping at his self-esteem and self-confidence.

- You may appear disinterested. If you actually are, it would be better to say so calmly.

- You may seem to have withdrawn your love. This impression would hit at the very heart of the relationship.

The things at stake, then, include emotional and physical health, confidence, trust, and security — factors that contribute to a wholesome personality.

It is primarily by example and experience that children learn to recognize and know the value of gentleness and reasonableness, justice and fairness, tolerance and patience. And it is by growing up under the protection of those who can be examples of such traits that the child is able to remain free from the stresses toward which this book is directed.

So the next time you find yourself raising your voice unintentionally — without legitimate need — pause long enough to take a deep breath. This is less painful than biting your tongue and requires less skill than counting to ten.

Not only will the deep breath interrupt the play of thoughts which has brought you to this unpleasant state in your feelings, but the breath will itself have a relaxing effect. If you deliberately take several slow, deep breaths, you can move a long way toward restoring your composure.

If in addition you tell yourself you are relaxing and that you are going to speak quietly, you may be astounded at the positive results — much as though someone is reading relaxation patter to you from this book.

But don't limit that quiet voice and calm manner only to your child. Try them also with your spouse or companion.

Whether or not men admit that in some ways they are still like little boys, most of them respond to gentleness and consideration — once they recover from the shock.

5.
How To Speak The Words

In reading the patter, speak slowly and distinctly.

Create an easy rhythm by pausing frequently between words. Pause at all commas and periods, and anywhere else that seems natural. Allow the pauses, as well as the words, to induce a relaxed feeling by their easy flow.

Remove all harshness and tenseness from your voice. Speak quietly, soothingly, and easily — not in a whisper, but no louder than necessary to be heard.

And speak with a certainty of the truth of your message.

The following is an example of proper pacing.

Example Patter

You are beginning now to be relaxed... becoming more and more relaxed... more relaxed and rested now... throughout your entire body... more relaxed and rested now... throughout your entire body... as all the strain is leaving now... all the tension is leaving now.

The suggested patter in each category is rather short, and often you will want to continue with one kind of corrective thought for a longer period. This is no problem. Merely repeat those phrases that seem to you to be most suitable and timely, and make up similar ones of your own.

There is nothing sacred about the patter in these pages. Your own good sense will guide you in forming other encouraging and healing phrases to use with your "patient."

Take your time. Do not rush your suggestions, and do not change abruptly into a statement that the person's subconscious mind will have difficulty accepting.

For instance, do not begin a treatment of illness by saying, "You are well."

Rather, as illustrated in the chapter on Health, start gradually and build up to that point, with phrases such as "You are beginning to return to good health now." Then follow with "becoming more and more (healthy, or balanced, or composed, etc.)."

Later you can say things like, "You are nearly well now, nearly completely cured now," if the illness is not too serious. For more entrenched problems, you may find it helpful to save the "nearly cured" remarks for follow-on sessions, as suggested below.

You can do no harm by being too optimistic and assertive in your statements, but your efforts will be wasted if you do not allow time for the patient's system to react gradually — both to accept the new idea and to make the change in the way it functions.

For simple matters, like relaxing, a few minutes is usually time enough. For more difficult tasks — such as restoring confidence or regenerating a better state of health, free from tension and worry — several minutes will probably be needed on a number of occasions, in an on-going program spread over several days or even weeks. At first you might use the treatment every day for a strong start. Later, if convenient, continue with perhaps two or three times a week.

When you have completed your suggestions in one category and wish to begin with another, just turn to that page and start reading. You may want to adjust the opening line or two to make a smooth transition into the new subject. Any words you find convenient will be all right, for the suggestions work best when they flow easily and naturally from your mouth.

You may return at any time to suggestions already given, either for re-emphasis or if you observe the desired effect has not been achieved.

It is a good idea to include throughout your patter a liberal sprinkling of "continuing to relax now, relaxing more and more now", so as to maintain the condition of peacefulness that is most receptive to your words.

Note strongly: It is essential that your words be clearly understood. This is particularly important with the word "not" or any other term that can reverse or distort the meaning.

Therefore, when you mean "can not," ***do not say "can't.""*** The sound of the "t" in the contraction is often lost completely, especially if the next word begins with "t" as in "can't talk" — but in any case is unable to carry the same emphasis as a distinctly spoken "not."

You may have heard someone seemingly shouting across a parking lot, "Did you say ***can*** or ***can***?" and getting an equally unclear answer. And or course, "can't" is not a word — merely a slovenly shortcut.

You have plenty of time — you will not be doing anything else as important right then as helping your child — so do not get careless.

Speak properly.

6.
Getting Started

Now, you may be getting ready to think up reasons why this approach cannot work for you.

Don't.

You would be wrong.

Instead, take that time you would have wasted on those negative thoughts and start practicing. At first when reading this material aloud, you are likely to feel self-conscious. That's normal. Don't let it throw you.

Read the patter over until you get the idea, until you become comfortable with the form of the repetition.

Then read it some more, so that you may speak slowly and easily, learning to pause between phrases. Pause where there are commas and anywhere that seems right, as you speak with rhythm, as you speak with calmness and certainty. Practice reading aloud to yourself, and then read aloud to someone else. Anyone, for practice.

Have a friend read some sections to you, so that you know they will work. Start with the relaxation (and of course, awakening) so that you experience the change in your muscles.

Then practice speaking the patter at odd moments of free time, to develop an easy flow of words. Talk aloud as you drive to the market. Talk aloud as you do the dishes or other routine work. And soon you will not need the book at all.

And that is as it should be. For deep within your own mind, you already know all that is said here.

Part II

What To Say

(The Basics)

to remove strain and tension,

restore emotional balance,

and eliminate fear and worry.

You can extend any patter

by repeating selected portions

or adding your own similar phrases.

7.
Relaxation

As you first begin, the emphasis is on establishing contact with the child in an easy manner and then initiating further relaxation. This latter objective is true even if the child is asleep. Sleep does not of itself indicate the body is relaxed. Many children sleep tensely, with mind distressed and body tensed or cramped.

The first task, then, is to induce a more calm state into the mind and relaxation into the body. The two conditions tend to go hand in hand, each having an effect upon the other. It is best, though, that both areas be treated specifically in an intermingled manner.

The following is an example of the approach to use.

If the child is asleep, begin speaking very quietly so as not to disturb him. If awake, skip the first two sentences of the patter and start right in on the message.

Note: Before starting, look ahead to the next chapter about what to say when finished — to close out the session in a professional manner.

Note also: In general, all treatment should begin with enough patter about relaxing to make the person more receptive to other suggestions.

REMEMBER: Speak slowly and use pauses as illustrated in the Example Patter in Chapter 5.

Patter for Relaxation

I'm going to speak to you very quietly now, without disturbing you. I'm going to speak very quietly so as not to disturb you.

You are beginning to relax now. You are beginning to relax now.

You are relaxing now, more and more. Your mind is relaxing, and your body is relaxing. Your mind is relaxing, and your body is relaxing.

Allow your mind to become more at ease now. Just allow your mind to become more and more at ease.

Your mind is becoming more and more at ease now. More and more at ease now. That's it.

All the strain is now dropping away. All the strain is now dropping away. And your mind is becoming more and more at ease now, more and more calm now.

Your body is becoming more relaxed and rested now. More relaxed and rested now.

You are beginning to relax now throughout your entire body. Relaxing throughout your entire body, as all the strain is leaving now, all the tension is leaving now.

(continued)

> Just relax and go with it now. Just relax and go with it now. That's it.
>
> So nice to relax now. So pleasant to rest now. That's it.

Remember to speak in an unhurried fashion, taking plenty of time. If you do it right, you will also relax yourself as you read aloud.

As you read, repeat any of the phrases whenever you wish — either immediately after first reading or later after other phrases.

You may extend the length of your patter as you judge advisable for implanting the new ideas firmly and comfortably into your patient's subconscious mind, so long as you don't make it a burden on either one of you.

8.
Closing And Awakening

Anytime you cease your instructions, it is best that you use some form of closing that makes it obvious to the patient that you are through.

Different circumstances call for different phrases. Accordingly, there are three general types of closing. In each session, you should select the kind most appropriate to that particular situation, as explained below.

For convenience, the three kinds are labeled:

- Simple Closing

- Awaken Now

- Awaken In The Morning

The simple closing is for occasions when your patient has retained full consciousness during the session. In these cases, a couple of phrases indicating you are finished is sufficient. You can use the example patter for Simple Closing as a guide.

However, as you continue your practice, and therefore become more proficient, you will find that as you relax your patient into a welcomed feeling of comfort, he may fall asleep or drop into a mild hypnotic state — which is simply a mental retiring into a sleep-like condition that is even more responsive to your suggestions. It is then usually a good idea to formally awaken him, rather than leave him alone to awaken by himself after a time.

(He will always awaken. The length of sleep will depend upon such things as fatigue and how well you induced the relaxation.)

For this purpose, you can employ the Awaken Now patter.

You can also use this patter anytime instead of the Simple Closing if you are unsure of whether the patient remained conscious. A fully relaxed patient, with eyes closed and breathing easily, looks much the same as one who has fallen asleep.

If the situation calls for the child or other patient to remain sleeping for a time, the Awaken In The Morning method is a good approach. This can be either for a normal night's sleep after a bedtime session, or for a shorter period at any time of the day — say, an hour or two — by adjustment of the wording.

These patters can be very effective when you read them quietly to a person already asleep when you begin. You may find it convenient — perhaps even necessary — to provide your help in this manner. In such cases, it is always beneficial to include suggestions about being in excellent condition upon awakening.

The example patters that follow for these three situations — still awake, awaken now, and awaken later — are representative of the words you might use.

Patter for Simple Closing

> You are now completely relaxed and refreshed and comfortable, and as I now stop speaking, you shall remain that way. As I now stop speaking, you shall remain that way, completely relaxed and refreshed and comfortable.

Be prepared to shift into one of the awakening patters if the patient seems not to respond. He may have fallen asleep.

But before assuming this to be the case, allow a few moments for the return to normal alertness. If the patient did fall asleep, a little more rest won't do any harm.

Some patients are reluctant to give up the marvelous and perhaps unaccustomed feeling of quiet peacefulness you have created, and may even feign an inability to respond. So be considerate and take your time. There is no need to rush an awakening.

Patter for Awaken Now

In a few moments, you shall awaken. You shall awaken, and shall be completely refreshed and full of energy. You shall remain relaxed and comfortable, and be completely refreshed and full of energy.

On the count of three, you shall awaken and feel perfectly wonderful.

On one, you are beginning to awaken now. Feeling the energy flowing through your body now. Feeling the energy flow throughout your entire system now.

Two, you are almost awake now. Almost awake now. Coming up now, completely refreshed, completely rested, feeling perfectly wonderful.

And now, on the count of three, you are wide awake. Wide awake, and eyes open.

You can adjust the pace of this patter — extending it as you judge best — by repeating some of the paragraphs or composing similar ones. Try to maintain a roughly equal interval between each count so the awakening goes smoothly, with no abrupt jumps.

If your patient fails to awaken promptly, do not be concerned. You have merely caused him to feel so comfortable where he is in his mind that he would rather stay there than awaken.

There is no such thing as sending him someplace from which he cannot return. You have merely relaxed his body, eased his mind, and made him feel good. He would like that state to continue.

Therefore, wait a few minutes and repeat the awakening exercise, counting up to five, or perhaps to ten, slowly, while reassuring him that as he awakens, he will feel perfectly wonderful.

And when he awakens, he will.

Patter for Awaken In The Morning

(or at some other time)

When you awaken in the morning, you will be completely refreshed and rested. You will be completely refreshed and rested, and you will feel perfectly wonderful.

You will have a new vitality, a new energy, a new healthy outlook on life, and you will feel perfectly wonderful.

When you awaken in the morning, you will feel perfectly wonderful.

You can change the wording to specify when you want the person to awaken. This might be at a specified time of day, or after a certain period, or when sufficiently rested.

9.
Emotional Balance

An essential part of a healthy child's make-up is calm emotions. Stresses upon the mind and body translate themselves into emotional disturbances.

In addition, many conditions are sensed directly with our emotions, so that they supply their own inputs. These may be either good or bad with respect to total body harmony.

Therefore, a prime requisite of successful therapy or of motherly attention is to ease the strains from the emotions. This is accomplished through quiet reassurance and positive direction.

The following statements are typical of the verbal patter that will bring about the result.

Patter for Emotional Balance

(after starting with relaxation)

Your emotions are now beginning to be more calm. They are beginning to be more calm. You are starting to feel better and better now, as you relax throughout your entire body.

You are feeling better and better now, as your emotions become more calm and you relax throughout your entire body.

All disturbances are leaving, and you are beginning to feel very good now. You are beginning to feel very good now. All disturbances are leaving, and you are beginning to feel very good now.

Feeling better and better now. Feeling better and better now. That's it.

10.
Fear And Worry

A child's life is frequently filled with events and situations that arouse fear. The act of growing up is a rather complicated process, and at times distressful, and a child's fancy paints all sorts of imagined circumstances that make him uneasy.

These may be surface and transient, such as concern about the new boy at school who is beginning to come across as a bully, or more deeply rooted fears, such as abandonment by parents and destruction by fire or terrorism.

Although a casual monologue of suggestive patter will not eliminate the deep causes of serious fears — at least not in a brief time — such patter can nevertheless reassure the child at a subconscious level and bring his emotions back to a fairly satisfactory state of harmony.

It is not necessary to have knowledge of specific problems to cause an improvement. The frequent repetition of statements to the effect that the fears and doubts are leaving will show striking results.

The following is an example of such statements. You can always add similar phrases about anxieties you know to be present.

Patter for Fear and Worry

(after starting with relaxation)

You are now becoming very much relaxed. You are becoming very much relaxed. And as you do, all worries and fears are dropping away. They are dropping away.

For there is nothing to worry about and nothing to fear. There is nothing to worry about and nothing to fear. For you are now completely safe. You are now completely secure.

All of your problems are leaving now. All of your problems are leaving now, as you relax more and more, and your mind becomes more and more at ease now. More and more at ease now. For there is nothing to worry about and nothing to fear. Nothing to worry about and nothing to fear.

Nothing negative can affect you in any way. Nothing negative can affect you in any way. For you are becoming more and more relaxed, more and more in balance.

As your mind relaxes, and your body relaxes. you are becoming more and more in balance now. More and more in harmony now.

And thus you will draw to yourself those things that are good for you. You will draw to yourself those situations that are good for you.

(continued)

All frustrations and anxieties are now passing from you. They are now passing from you, as your worries and fears are leaving now. They are leaving now. They are leaving now.

For you know that there is nothing to worry about and nothing to fear. There is nothing to worry about and nothing to fear.

Part III

What To Say

(For Health)

to maintain or restore general health,

reduce discouragement and sorrow,

increase resistance to disease,

and treat specific difficulties.

You can extend any patter

by repeating selected portions

or adding your own similar phrases.

Note:

In general, all treatments should begin with

enough patter about relaxing to make the

person more receptive to other suggestions.

11.
General Health

A child's body, when free from negative influences, arranges for the maintenance of its own good health. Unless there is some serious problem, a reminder to the subconscious that it has the capacity to maintain perfect health should show good results.

The same approach can be used for restoring health, with minor changes in wording to aid with improvement.

Also of importance is the stressing of the metaphysical truth that we draw to ourselves that which we are and that which we believe.

Therefore, in the next two patters — for maintaining and restoring good health — the emphasis is upon drawing to the child those things needed for that result.

You can add to this wording (or replace it with) suggestions about improving the effectiveness of the immune system, as in the third patter in this chapter. Repeat your own phrases in this same manner.

For specific problems, refer to later topics.

Patter for Maintaining Health

(after starting with relaxation)

Now as you become more and more harmonized throughout your entire body, your mind is keeping your body in perfect health. Your mind is maintaining your body in perfect health.

For when the body is relaxed and rested, when the body is harmonized and in tune, as it is now, when all the parts of the body are rested and working properly, as it is now, then you are in perfect health. Then you are in perfect health.

And you are now maintaining that state of perfect health. Each day you are returning to that state of harmony which is perfect health.

When you remain in harmony, you are drawing to yourself all those things that are necessary to maintain your perfect health. You are drawing to yourself those things needed for perfect health.

They are flowing toward you now. They are flowing toward you now, and will continue to flow, as you become more relaxed, and more rested, and more in harmony.

(continued)

And with each passing day, those things you need for perfect health will continue to flow toward you. They will continue to move toward you, for you are attracting them to yourself. You are attracting them to yourself because you are now in harmony. You are now in tune.

Nothing that is negative can now affect you. Nothing that is negative in any way, no thought and no person that is negative in any way, can now affect you. Nothing negative can now affect you.

Therefore you shall no longer get sick. You shall no longer get sick, for you shall be in perfect health. No more shall you ever get sick, for you shall be in perfect health, and sickness can not touch you. It can not touch you.

You are becoming so much in harmony, and so in tune, that sickness can not touch you. You can never become sick.

And you will remain in perfect health throughout your entire life. You will remain in perfect health your entire life.

Patter for Restoring Health

(after starting with relaxation)

As you become more and more harmonized throughout your entire body, your mind is returning your body to perfect health. Your mind is returning your body to perfect health.

For when the body is relaxed and rested, when the body is harmonized and in tune, when all the parts of the body are rested and working properly, then you are in perfect health. Then you are in perfect health.

And you are now returning to that perfect health. You are returning to that state of harmony which is perfect health.

You are now beginning to draw to yourself all those things which are necessary for perfect health. You are beginning to draw to yourself those things needed for perfect health.

They are beginning to flow toward you now. They are beginning to flow toward you now, as you become more relaxed, and more rested, and more in harmony.

And with each passing day, those things you need for perfect health will continue to flow toward you. They will continue to more toward you, for you are attracting them to yourself.

(continued)

You are attracting them to yourself, because you are now in harmony. You are now in tune.

Nothing negative can now affect you. Nothing that is negative in any way, no thought and no person that is negative in any way can now affect you. Nothing negative can now affect you.

Everything that is necessary for the physical body, for the emotions, and for the mind to become in perfect health shall move toward you, shall be drawn to you. Everything physical and non-physical, everything emotional and mental that is needed for your environment is now moving toward you, is being drawn to you.

And thus, with each passing day, you shall become more and more healthy, more and more in harmony, more and more in perfect tune. You shall become more and more in perfect tune.

Patter for Improving the Immune System

(after starting with relaxation)

As you become more and more relaxed, your immune system is improving. It is improving now, and will continue to improve, more and more.

Your immune system is beginning to work more effectively now. It is beginning to work more effectively now, and making you more resistant to disease. Making you more resistant now, more resistant to disease of any kind. That's it.

Your are becoming more resistant to disease of any kind. And that improvement will continue. It will continue, improving more and more.

And as it improves, it is combating any disease you may already have. It is casting off any disease you may already have.

So you are becoming more healthy now, more and more healthy now. That's it.

12.
Pain And Ache

Many simple aches and pains, and sometimes even more excruciating agonies, can be removed or alleviated by a beginner through the repetition of suitable phrases. (Of course, all pain can be eliminated by a person of sufficient skill.)

The easiest pains to remove are those caused by tension or strains in the muscles, since they disappear as a consequence to relaxation.

In a somewhat similar category are the aches a child will develop from being confined too long in bed from illness or injury. Here the question of proper circulation may be involved, and suggestions about improvement of circulation can be very helpful.

Headaches are often the result of mental stresses and physical tensions in the neck muscles that reduce circulation to the brain, and for these a simple relaxation patter can be quite effective. However, you can attack the problem more directly by adjusting the wording to include phrases about removing the headache.

Patter for Pain

(after starting with relaxation)

The pain is beginning to leave now. The pain is beginning to leave now. It is hurting less and less. It is hurting less and less, and you are beginning to feel better now.

The pain is going away, and you are beginning to feel better now.

You are feeling better now. You are feeling better now, as all the pain is leaving, and all the hurt is flowing away. It is flowing away.

The hurt is flowing away, and you are feeling better now, feeling more comfortable now, feeling more relaxed now.

Patter for Ache

The ache is beginning to leave now. The ache is beginning to leave now. It is aching less and less now, bothering less and less now.

The circulation is beginning to improve, and the ache is flowing away now. It is flowing away now, as the blood begins to move more freely through that area, as the circulation improves in that area. The circulation is improving in that area.

The ache is flowing away now, leaving you feeling more comfortable, more at ease.

You are feeling better now, feeling more comfortable, as the circulation continues to improve, and as your muscles relax more and more.

The ache is leaving, and you are feeling better now. You are feeling better now.

13.
Speedy Recovery

Patter for a quicker and easier recovery is much like the wording for restoring health, but shifts the emphasis to that particular goal, as in this example.

As always, when changing the direction of your phrases from one objective — say, eliminating pain or anxiety — to another, it is a good idea to work into the new suggestions gradually, by indicating the desired new condition "is now beginning."

You can extend and vary the transition as you think suitable, with a bit more in the first session and less in later ones.

Patter for Speedy Recovery

(after starting with relaxation)

You are beginning now to make a more speedy recovery. Your mind is arranging a more speedy recovery, through its complete control of your entire system.

Your mind is now causing a quicker recovery, a more speedy recovery. It is causing a quicker recovery as you return back to perfect health.

You are returning now more quickly to full recovery and perfect health. That's it.

You are beginning to feel better now, as you move more easily toward perfect health, moving more quickly to complete health.

As you continue to become even more relaxed, and more rested, you are making a more speedy recovery.

You are returning to full health more quickly now, more easily now, and soon will be full recovered. That's it.

You shall quickly become more and more healthy, more and more in harmony, as you move easily and quickly toward a full recovery.

14.
Digestion

Good digestion is just a portion of overall good health and is closely tied to strain and emotions. It is aided by any suggestions that help in those areas.

In addition, you can give specific suggestions about the digestion process and the absorbing of food to form body tissue and energy.

In some cases, an upset stomach is tied closely to a headache, and the two and can be treated together.

The digestion patter on the following page is a variation of the phrases offered earlier for restoring general health. You can similarly devise your own suggestions.

Patter for Digestion

You are continuing now to relax, and are feeling even better. Feeling even better now. Relaxing even more now. And as you do, all the parts of your body are beginning to work perfectly now. All the glands and organs throughout your entire body are beginning to work perfectly now.

And the stomach is working perfectly now. The stomach is working perfectly. It is digesting the food now, digesting it better and better, digesting the food perfectly now, so that all you need from the food is now flowing into the body.

Everything you need to draw from the food is flowing into your body, to bring you perfect health. Flowing into your body, to give you perfect health.

All the different parts of the food that you need for perfect health are now moving into your body.

They are moving into your body now. More and more perfectly now. That's it.

And your body is absorbing the food. Your body is absorbing the food, and rebuilding itself. The bones are rebuilding, and the muscles are rebuilding, and the nerves are rebuilding.

(continued)

All the various parts of the body are rebuilding now. Building more and more strongly now. Building more and more healthily now. That's it.

Bringing to you now perfect health and perfect harmony. Bringing to you perfect health and perfect body tone. More and more, throughout the entire body now, bringing perfect health and perfect body tone. That's it.

Just relax and go with it now. Just relax and enjoy it now.

15.
Allergies, Rashes, And Warts

With all matters of health, the earlier patter for improving it can often prove beneficial, as can wording to improve the immune system. Some allergies and skin problems may be helped by additional phrases tailored more specifically to those areas.

For example, warts are susceptible to shrinking and removal by simple suggestion, and rashes can sometimes be quickly removed or made less bothersome.

Of course, you should never forego medical treatment when needed.

But it will do no harm to try the method on "cosmetic" or other conditions — like, say, hickeys — that, while perhaps distressing, are no great threat to health.

You can use the following patters as guides. Stretch out the treatment by repeating some of the phrases or using your own.

Patter for Allergies

(after starting with relaxation)

*** You can supplement the following phrases with earlier ones about improving the immune system.*

Your allergy is beginning to be less bothersome now. It is becoming less bothersome now as your body begins to overcome it.

The allergy symptoms are beginning to leave now. They are leaving now. The symptoms are going away now as the allergy weakens, as your body overcomes it.

Your resistance to the allergy is building. Your resistance is strengthening now, as your mind instructs your body on how to fight it. Your resistance is strengthening now.

And so the allergy is becoming less of a problem, less and less bothersome now, as the symptoms are going away.

The symptoms are going away, and will not return. You are recovering from the allergy. You are recovering, and the allergy will not return.

Patter for Rashes or Warts

(after starting with relaxation)

*** Insert "rash," "wart," or other word in the blank.*

As all tension leaves, your mind is able to control your body more effectively, able to control your entire system more effectively, and it is starting to do that now. It is starting to do that now, controlling your health more completely, attacking your health problems more strongly.

And therefore your mind can cure your (___). It is able to cure your (___) by controlling your system more effectively, and it is working to do that now. It is starting to do that now. That's it.

Your mind is beginning to do whatever is necessary to cure your (___), doing everything needed to remove your (___). And therefore it is being cured.

Your mind is working now to remove your (___), working to cure your (___). And therefore it will go away. It is going away. Your (___) is being cured.

As your entire system becomes more effective, it is getting rid of your (___). It is getting rid of this condition. As your health system becomes more effective, it is getting rid of this condition. It is curing your (___).

(continued)

And therefore your (___) will disappear. It will disappear and not return, for your system is throwing off your problem.

Your mind will continue to improve your health and cure this condition, so your (___) will disappear. It will disappear and will not return.

16.
Discouragement

It is obvious that the right kind of patter will help to overcome discouragement, since it is no more nor less than a pep talk. However, it is a pep talk that is carefully planned to instill confidence and encouragement in the subconscious mind, rather than the conscious.

The pep talk for discouragement is delivered calmly, as simple statements of fact, instead of emotionally to arouse. And it concentrates most strongly upon what is happening now in the child's mind, and only secondarily upon what will occur when he returns to the fray.

Also unlike a sports team pep talk, which is all about the future — the next play or tomorrow's game — the emphasis here is initially upon phrases using the present tense, like "Your discouragement is leaving now," and "You are becoming more confident.". Later it shifts to the past tense to note success, as with "All discouragement has left."

The following patter is one approach.

Patter for Discouragement

(after starting with relaxation)

As your mind becomes at ease now, all negative thoughts are leaving. All discouraging thoughts are leaving. They are leaving now. They are leaving now.

All discouragement is leaving now, as you become more and more relaxed, more and more at ease. All discouragement is vanishing now, as your mind becomes free from strain and free from worry. All discouragement is leaving.

And you are becoming more cheerful now. Becoming more gay and cheerful now. Becoming encouraged now, as all negativity is leaving, and you become more positive and more cheerful.

Your discouragement has left now, and your confidence is increasing. Your confidence is now increasing, and you are becoming more encouraged and more cheerful.

You are no longer discouraged, and with each passing day you will grow more confident and more cheerful. You will continue to be more encouraged and more cheerful.

17.
Sorrow

Occasional sorrow is a normal condition of life, but if it is too deep or prolonged, it can affect health and behavior, with symptoms such as lack of interest or energy, or serious depression.

While these symptoms may be aided by phrases similar to those for general health and discouragement, the sorrow itself doesn't lend itself to treatment by a standard patter.

Sorrow is always a very personal matter, varying with the specific cause and surrounding circumstances, and you need to select your suggestions carefully so they are appropriate to the situation.

Sorrow from the death of a family member is different from that caused by a lost love, or the anguish of a mass killing by terrorists, or a grievous disappointment in one's fondest hopes. It may also be accompanied by a false sense of guilt, as a child may feel from parental divorce or injury to a sibling.

Your objective should be a form of counseling. This may involve trying to alleviate feelings of emotional pain, depression, and insecurity while offering suitable reassurance.

In picking your phrases, recognize they will reflect your own beliefs about dealing with sorrow unless you choose to lay them aside.

Patter for Sorrow

(after starting with relaxation)

***** The wording for sorrow must be tailored to the individual case.*

One way to compose your patter is to select phrases from other topics and adjust them slightly to be specific to your situation.

Or you can start from scratch, using a similar manner of wording.

Remember always to speak slowly and calmly, and avoid sermonizing or lecturing.

Part IV

What To Say

(For Attitude And Behavior)

to build confidence and resolve,

adjust attitudes and prejudices,

and resist pressure for wrong

or self-harming behavior.

You can extend any patter

by repeating selected portions

or adding your own similar phrases.

Note:

In general, all treatments should begin with

enough patter about relaxing to make the

person more receptive to other suggestions.

18.
Confidence

The treatment for improving confidence is much the same in principle as for removing fear and worry, since anxiety or doubt is the major cause of lack of confidence.

It may not appear to be so — people often forget or have never understood what caused them to be so sure they cannot do something — but in most cases the building of confidence must be coupled to the removal of (1) concern about the result or (2) a more general, all-pervading discouragement or tension.

The following patter is representative of an approach that might be used on children of perhaps eight years and older, or whenever they begin to decry their lack of ability. And of course, for an adult of any age.

You can substitute simpler phrases for younger children, anything that will reassure them that they are capable. Depending upon the situation, you might want to include statements about patience and freedom from frustration, and possibly the thought that they should not judge their results too harshly,

However, avoid any statement that would suggest that the child should not expect very much of himself. This could have the opposite effect to the one you want.

Patter for Confidence

(after starting with relaxation)

You are beginning now to be more confident. You are beginning to be more confident. As you relax completely, and your mind becomes free from strain and stress, you are becoming more confident.

You are becoming more sure of yourself. Your confidence is building now, more and more, as you become more sure of yourself. Your confidence is building as you become more sure of yourself.

For you know you can do well those things you decide to do. You know you can accomplish those things you set out to do.

And as your mind now becomes more at ease, and more rested, you are beginning to experience that confidence. You are experiencing that confidence. And you know that you are very capable.

You are experiencing that confidence, and you know that you are very capable.

19.
Studies

The relationship between strain or disturbance and poor concentration is well known. The first rule for studying effectively or taking an examination is to become relaxed.

The following patter is directed toward that purpose, by including the building of confidence in the child's ability to do well in his studies.

The wording is intended to encourage. Be careful not to change it into a lecture or reprimand.

Patter for Studies

(after starting with relaxation)

And now, as you are relaxed and rested, your mind is becoming more clear and more organized. Your mind is becoming more clear and more organized, as all strain, all stress, all confusion have left it now. All stress and all confusion have left it now.

And therefore, your mind is now more organized. Your mind is more alert now, and more able to perform well.

And consequently, anything you study will be easier for you now. All of your studies will be easier for you now. They will be easier for you. For your mind is becoming more free from strain and more organized.

You will find new interest in your studies, and new excitement. You will find new challenge in your studies, for they will be easier for you now, and will become more meaningful.

Your studies will become easier, and more interesting and meaningful. They will be more meaningful for you now, as your mind becomes relaxed and rested, free from strain and interference. They will be easier for you now, as your mind becomes free from interference.

(continued)

For you have a good mind. You have a good mind, and you are able to learn your studies well. You are able to learn them well, and are now beginning to be able to learn them more and more easily.

You have a good mind, and are now beginning to be able to do your studies more and more easily.

20.
Tasks

It takes no great insight to recognize that a relaxed and cheerful child is more likely to perform his assigned tasks and duties than that same child if strained or disturbed.

The main emphasis here is on relaxation and removal of negativity.

The other words point toward the objective of getting the work done. Avoid any statements that might appear to be reprimands or indicate hostility.

Patter for Tasks

And now, as you relax throughout your entire body, with all strain gone, so also are all negative thoughts dropping away. All negative reactions are dropping away, dropping away completely. All thoughts of unpleasantness of any kind are dropping away completely.

And it now becomes easier for you to do whatever must be done. It becomes easier for you to understand why things must be done. It becomes easier and easier for you to be sympathetic to why things must be done.

Therefore, as you do your work, as you do your daily tasks, as you do those jobs which must be done, they will become easier and easier for you to do. They will become more pleasant for you to do, easier and more pleasant for you.

No longer will you react negatively when asked to do your tasks. No longer will you react negatively, for all negativity has left you now.

All negativity has left you now, and you are completely relaxed and completely composed, and you recognize that it will be easier and easier for you to do your tasks. It will now be easier for you to do your work.

(continued)

You will find yourself looking forward to completing your tasks. You will find yourself looking forward to completing them, wanting to do them, so you can have the satisfaction of a job well done. Looking forward to doing them, for the satisfaction of a job well done.

And as you do your tasks, you will feel pride in your work. You will take pride in your work, for a job well done.

21.
Public Speaking Or Appearances

Concern or anxiety about appearing before groups, such as for public speaking, court testimony, or important meetings — or even job interviews — can be reduced by any phrases that build confidence and eliminate worry. In some cases it may be appropriate to deal also with discouragement. Patters for all these topics are in earlier chapters.

Your suggestions will be most effective if you adjust the phrasing to mention the particular event or situation that is now, or will soon be, causing the stress.

Your main approach should be directed toward relaxation and comfort, plus statements that the person will remain fully at ease throughout the event.

The following patter is designed for public speaking, but can be used for other situations with minor changes in the wording.

Patter for Public Speaking

(after starting with relaxation)

As the time approaches for you to speak, you will find yourself becoming fully relaxed. When it is time for you to speak, you will be fully relaxed.

Before you begin, any anxiety you may have been feeling will have gone away. Any concern about your performance will have gone away.

You will be confident in your performance, at ease during your performance, and therefore your mind will remain clear. Your mind will remain clear, so you can think and speak well. You will think and speak well.

You will have no anxiety at any time, and will respond to questions or comments in a professional manner. You will respond to any questions or comments confidently, in a professional manner.

22.
Relationships With People

Freedom from strain is a tremendous aid in dealing with people of all kinds, in any circumstance, for it allows the mind to remain clear and the personality to be expressed naturally.

In addition, a relaxed mind becomes more receptive to suggestions for reducing racial, religious, or other types of prejudices, although these are hard to alter when well entrenched.

The following two approaches for these related areas — (a) general improvement of relationships and (b) reduction of prejudices — may prove rewarding.

Patter for Relationships with People

(after starting with relaxation)

For general improvement

And now, as all strain and concern have left, as you are feeling more emotionally composed, you will be able to deal with other people more easily. You will begin to deal with other people more easily.

In days ahead, as you continue to be more emotionally composed, you will be able to deal with other people more easily. You realize that you will be able to deal with other people more easily, and more naturally.

Therefore your relationships with other people will be improving now. They will be improving now. They will improve, and you will be able to deal with all people more easily and naturally.

You will find yourself knowing how to respond, and what to say, and what to do, more easily now. You will know what to do.

You will be able to be yourself more comfortably now. You will be yourself more comfortably.

(continued)

You will find yourself becoming more friendly now, more at ease now, as you do things with other people, as you spend time with other people. For you will remain relaxed. You will remain relaxed and emotionally composed.

And therefore people will like you better, as you become more friendly. They will like you better.

And your relationships with other people will continue to get better and better now. They will continue to grow better.

For reducing prejudices

As you think more clearly now, you will begin to realize that your prejudices are harming you. Your prejudices are harming you in your relationships with people.

You will recognize that your prejudices are bad for you, because they impair your judgments about other people, and interfere with sensible behavior and good relationships.

You are beginning to recognize that your prejudices about (___) are not well founded. They are not well founded, and are interfering with intelligent behavior and pleasant relationships.

You do not want prejudices about (___) interfering with intelligent behavior or your relationships. Therefore your prejudices will begin to go away. They will begin to go away. You do not want your prejudices to interfere, so they will begin to go away.

Your prejudices will become weaker and weaker, and gradually go away. They will gradually go away.

As they continue to grow weaker, they will eventually go away completely. They will eventually go away completely.

(continued)

Your relationships with people will continue to improve and become better and better. Your relationships with people will continue to improve.

You will be able to relate to people more easily now, and deal with them more comfortably. You will relate to people more comfortably.

23.
Clear Thinking

Any significant stress — from a work situation, financial burden, emotional disturbance, conflict with peers, or other reason — can be destructive of clear thinking. That's why most of us have to withdraw to a quiet place now and then, if only in our mind, to recover composure and try to sort things out or weigh the merits of decisions.

Whether child, teenager, or adult, a person has the best chance to think clearly when free from stress.

Patter of the following general kind can be helpful, but it will be more effective if you tailor it to the person or situation.

You might include statements about such things as not being too hasty in making a decision, or too quick to judge, or needing to carefully evaluate situations or events before acting, and possible consequences of usual behavior.

Patter for Clear Thinking

(after starting with relaxation)

As you become free from strain, your mind can function more effectively, more efficiently. It is beginning to do that now, beginning to work more effectively now, allowing you to think more clearly. That's it.

You are beginning to think more clearly now. You are beginning to think more clearly now, as your mind works more effectively, more clearly.

That's it. You are thinking more clearly now, and will continue to do so. You will continue to think more clearly.

With each passing day your thinking will become more clear, more sharp. Your mind will process your thoughts more capably, more efficiently. With each passing day your thinking will be more efficient and more clear.

And therefore, in any situation, you will find yourself knowing how to respond, and what to say, and what to do, more easily now. You will have better insight into people and know what to say and what to do.

You will think through all problems more easily now and know what to do. You will think through your problems more easily and know what to do.

24.
Standing Alone
Against Peer Pressure

Many of the problems a teen-ager — or anyone else — may face arise from pressure to conform to someone else's expectations or demands, whether real or imagined. The distinction is academic, because it is the impression in the mind of the individual feeling the pressure that determines the reality and seriousness of the problem.

You may be familiar with some youngster's desperate cry — perhaps your own in years past — *"But you don't understand!"*

The following patter is intended to help a person become more self-reliant and less susceptible to group or individual pressure.

See also the chapters for avoiding smoking and drugs.

Patter for Standing Alone

(after starting with relaxation)

You are becoming more secure now. You are becoming more secure now, and more confident. Becoming more secure and confident now, and more able to make your own decisions. That's it.

As you become more confident, you will begin now to rely more on your own decisions. You will rely more on your own decisions, deciding what is right for you, deciding what is best for you.

As you continue to gain confidence, with your mind free from strain, you will think more clearly, and trust your own judgment more. You will trust you own judgment more.

You will trust your own judgment, and will not allow others to talk you into doing something that is bad for you. You will not allow others to pressure you into doing something that is wrong or bad for you.

And you are now able to think more clearly. You are able to think more clearly, and your feeling of self-worth is growing. Your awareness of self-worth is growing, and you will not allow others to pressure you into doing anything bad for you.

(continued)

As your awareness of self-worth grows, the need to belong to a group is lessening. The need to belong to a group is lessening now. The need to be a follower is lessening now. That's it.

And as this recognition of your self-worth continues to grow, you are becoming more able to decide whether a friend or a group is good for you. You are more able to decide for yourself whether a friend or group is good for you.

You are more able to decide whether to join the group or go your own way. And you are more able to act on your decision, and be more comfortable with your decision. You are able to make a better decision and be comfortable with it.

And therefore, when you have to make a decision about what to do, you will find yourself using your own good judgment, more and more, and not being influenced by the pressure of a friend or group. You will use your own good judgment, and not be influenced by pressure.

You can stand alone now. You can stand alone now, and will not allow others to talk you into ___ (smoking, drinking, doing something that is bad for you, something you know is wrong).

You can stand alone now, and will not allow others to talk you into (___). You will not allow others to pressure you into doing anything wrong or anything bad for you.

25.
Avoiding Smoking

This topic can be a bit tricky. The assumption with most therapy is that the patient is a willing recipient of the suggestions, as in the case of an adult patient wishing to quit smoking.

If you are trying to help your child avoid starting to smoke, but the youngster insists on doing it, you will probably need to be subtle in introducing this patter — unless the child is so relaxed as to not care or has fallen asleep.

You might blend some of the following wording with other sections about clear thinking, standing alone, or avoiding drugs.

If the person has already been smoking for a while and you want to stop this practice before the habit takes hold more strongly, you can alter the wording to include reasons for quitting — reasons that are important to your subject, not just to you.

Patter for Avoiding Smoking

(after starting with relaxation)

As you continue to relax, you realize your health is import to you. You recognize that your good health is very important to you.

And you know smoking is bad for your health. You know smoking is bad for your health, and bad for your future.

You realize you don't want to harm yourself by smoking. You don't wish to harm yourself or jeopardize your future by smoking. You don't want to harm yourself, so you will resist smoking. You will continue to resist smoking.

Therefore, as your confidence continues to grow each day, you will not allow others to talk you into smoking. You will not allow anyone to pressure you into smoking.

You will not allow anyone to force you, or ridicule you, or shame you into smoking. Your confidence is growing, and you will not allow anyone to challenge you, or shame you, into smoking.

26.
Avoiding Drugs

At an appallingly young age, children become exposed to pressures that may lead them into experimenting with the use of drugs. Anything you can do to strengthen your child's resistance to these pressures will improve his chance of growing up without falling prey to the drug habit.

The approach here should be multiple, covering such areas as:

- Eliminating feelings of insecurity

- Building self-confidence

- Lessening of need to join the crowd

- Standing alone among his peers when disproving of their actions

Words of the following sort might be very helpful. They could be the factor that would swing the child toward abstinence in a moment of decision under stress.

Patter for Avoiding Drugs

(after starting with relaxation)

You are becoming more secure now. You are becoming more confident and secure now, and more able to make your own decisions. You are secure enough to stand alone, to stand against the crowd.

Therefore you will trust your own judgment, and will not allow others to talk you into using harmful drugs. You will not allow anyone to pressure you into the use of dangerous drugs.

You are secure enough now to stand alone. You know the danger of harmful drugs, the danger to your health and your future, and will not allow anyone to force you, or ridicule you, or shame you into using dangerous drugs.

No one can challenge you, or shame you, into using drugs. No one can challenge you, or shame you, into using drugs.

For you are able to make your own decisions, and the recognition that you can make good decisions is growing. And therefore no one can push you into using drugs. No one can push you into the use of drugs.

27.
Tenderness

You probably noticed the point made throughout the book — that the suggestions could be helpful not only to children, but to anyone else in your household as well. And that is certainly true.

None of this material is restricted to children. It applies equally to everyone. The general approach is universal.

Of course, as you become more familiar with the patter and more confident in its use, you will adjust your words to the particular patient and his needs.

This last topic is directed more toward adults. If you like tenderness and affection in your daily diet, you might test out the following on the man or woman in your life.

Patter for Tenderness

(after starting with relaxation)

You are becoming more gentle now. You are becoming more gentle now, more gentle and tender. You are becoming more gentle and tender now, as you relax completely.

All strain is leaving now, all harshness is leaving now, and you are becoming more gentle and more tender.

All tension is leaving now, all strain is leaving, and you can feel the tenderness beginning to flow through you. The tenderness is beginning to flow through you. That's it.

All hardness is leaving now. All hardness is leaving now, as you feel the gentleness flowing through you. Just relax and enjoy the feeling now. Just relax and enjoy the feeling. That's it.

As you become more gentle, your affection is coming to the surface. Your affection is coming to the surface. You are feeling more tender now, and your affection is becoming more open now. It is becoming more open now.

You are becoming more tender and more openly affectionate, more gentle and affectionate now. Becoming more gentle and affectionate.

That's it.

About the Author

The author's experience covers 50 years of research, writing, and teaching in engineering, psychic, and mental therapy fields. He holds a BS in Industrial Engineering from Stanford University ('51), an MBA from Pepperdine University ('76), and mind behavior degrees of Doctor of Metaphysics and Doctor of Hypnotherapy. His 1960 text *Digital Computer Principles* was used in 14 colleges.

Professional training in hypnosis during college resulted 15 years later in teaching himself, by experimenting, to obtain psychic information skillfully. He then developed an instructional method for this skill, which he named Directed Intuition, and taught numerous classes. These achievements led to his degrees in mind behavior.

In 1971-72, in a temporary departure from aerospace and computer engineering, he offered professional therapy and counseling, combining hypnosis with psychic sensing and healing. This period saw the first publishing of *Mother, Heal Your Child*, which was expanded into this Third Edition in 2003.

In '72 the author began the task of converting his psychic sensing course and related material into a self-training manual. His extensive experiences with patients and associates in the '70s had added so great a number of case studies and incidents to his insightful knowledge about psychic healing and problems traceable to past lifetimes — far beyond the scope of a single cohesive book — that it became necessary to divide these subjects into three volumes in an integrated set.

The training manual for Directed Intuition was published in 2002 under the title *Learning the Psychic Shift*. With the other two books, soon to be published, the set covers (1) practical uses for psychic sensing, (2) problems arising from circumstances in previous lifetimes, and (3) techniques for psychic healing.